The Usernames and Passwords Book

Keep Track, Stay Organized

Amy Sagan

ISBN: 1724865013
ISBN-13: 978-1724865014

IMPORTANT:

**Please keep this book
safe and secure.**

**Your usernames and passwords
should always be kept confidential.**

Category:

Website:

URL:

USERNAME	PASSWORD

Website:

URL:

USERNAME	PASSWORD

Website:

URL:

USERNAME	PASSWORD

Website:

URL:

USERNAME	PASSWORD

Category:

Website:

URL:

USERNAME	PASSWORD

Website:

URL:

USERNAME	PASSWORD

Website:

URL:

USERNAME	PASSWORD

Website:

URL:

USERNAME	PASSWORD

Category:

Website:

URL:

USERNAME	PASSWORD

Website:

URL:

USERNAME	PASSWORD

Website:

URL:

USERNAME	PASSWORD

Website:

URL:

USERNAME	PASSWORD

Category:

Website:

URL:

USERNAME	PASSWORD

Website:

URL:

USERNAME	PASSWORD

Website:

URL:

USERNAME	PASSWORD

Website:

URL:

USERNAME	PASSWORD

Category:

Website:

URL:

USERNAME	PASSWORD

Website:

URL:

USERNAME	PASSWORD

Website:

URL:

USERNAME	PASSWORD

Website:

URL:

USERNAME	PASSWORD

Category:

Website:

URL:

USERNAME	PASSWORD

Website:

URL:

USERNAME	PASSWORD

Website:

URL:

USERNAME	PASSWORD

Website:

URL:

USERNAME	PASSWORD

Category:

Website:

URL:

USERNAME	PASSWORD

Website:

URL:

USERNAME	PASSWORD

Website:

URL:

USERNAME	PASSWORD

Website:

URL:

USERNAME	PASSWORD

Category:

FINANCIAL, SOCIAL MEDIA, SHOPPING, ETC.

Website:

URL:

USERNAME	PASSWORD

Website:

URL:

USERNAME	PASSWORD

Website:

URL:

USERNAME	PASSWORD

Website:

URL:

USERNAME	PASSWORD

Category:

Website:

URL:

USERNAME	PASSWORD

Website:

URL:

USERNAME	PASSWORD

Website:

URL:

USERNAME	PASSWORD

Website:

URL:

USERNAME	PASSWORD

Category:

FINANCIAL, SOCIAL MEDIA, SHOPPING, ETC

Website:

URL:

USERNAME	PASSWORD

Website:

URL:

USERNAME	PASSWORD

Website:

URL:

USERNAME	PASSWORD

Website:

URL:

USERNAME	PASSWORD

Category:

Website:

URL:

USERNAME	PASSWORD

Website:

URL:

USERNAME	PASSWORD

Website:

URL:

USERNAME	PASSWORD

Website:

URL:

USERNAME	PASSWORD

Category:

Website:

URL:

USERNAME	PASSWORD

Website:

URL:

USERNAME	PASSWORD

Website:

URL:

USERNAME	PASSWORD

Website:

URL:

USERNAME	PASSWORD

Category:

Website:

URL:

USERNAME	PASSWORD

Website:

URL:

USERNAME	PASSWORD

Website:

URL:

USERNAME	PASSWORD

Website:

URL:

USERNAME	PASSWORD

Category:

Website:

URL:

USERNAME	PASSWORD

Website:

URL:

USERNAME	PASSWORD

Website:

URL:

USERNAME	PASSWORD

Website:

URL:

USERNAME	PASSWORD

Category:

Website:

URL:

USERNAME	PASSWORD

Website:

URL:

USERNAME	PASSWORD

Website:

URL:

USERNAME	PASSWORD

Website:

URL:

USERNAME	PASSWORD

Category:

FINANCIAL, SOCIAL MEDIA, SHOPPING, ETC

Website:

URL:

USERNAME	PASSWORD

Website:

URL:

USERNAME	PASSWORD

Website:

URL:

USERNAME	PASSWORD

Website:

URL:

USERNAME	PASSWORD

Category:

Website:

URL:

USERNAME	PASSWORD

Website:

URL:

USERNAME	PASSWORD

Website:

URL:

USERNAME	PASSWORD

Website:

URL:

USERNAME	PASSWORD

Category:

FINANCIAL, SOCIAL MEDIA, SHOPPING, ETC

Website:

URL:

USERNAME	PASSWORD

Website:

URL:

USERNAME	PASSWORD

Website:

URL:

USERNAME	PASSWORD

Website:

URL:

USERNAME	PASSWORD

Category:

Website:

URL:

USERNAME	PASSWORD

Website:

URL:

USERNAME	PASSWORD

Website:

URL:

USERNAME	PASSWORD

Website:

URL:

USERNAME	PASSWORD

Category:

Website:

URL:

USERNAME	PASSWORD

Website:

URL:

USERNAME	PASSWORD

Website:

URL:

USERNAME	PASSWORD

Website:

URL:

USERNAME	PASSWORD

Category:

Website:

URL:

USERNAME	PASSWORD

Website:

URL:

USERNAME	PASSWORD

Website:

URL:

USERNAME	PASSWORD

Website:

URL:

USERNAME	PASSWORD

Category:

Website:

URL:

USERNAME	PASSWORD

Website:

URL:

USERNAME	PASSWORD

Website:

URL:

USERNAME	PASSWORD

Website:

URL:

USERNAME	PASSWORD

Category:

Website:

URL:

USERNAME	PASSWORD

Website:

URL:

USERNAME	PASSWORD

Website:

URL:

USERNAME	PASSWORD

Website:

URL:

USERNAME	PASSWORD

Category:

FINANCIAL, SOCIAL MEDIA, SHOPPING, ETC

Website:

URL:

USERNAME	PASSWORD

Website:

URL:

USERNAME	PASSWORD

Website:

URL:

USERNAME	PASSWORD

Website:

URL:

USERNAME	PASSWORD

Category:

Website:

URL:

USERNAME	PASSWORD

Website:

URL:

USERNAME	PASSWORD

Website:

URL:

USERNAME	PASSWORD

Website:

URL:

USERNAME	PASSWORD

www.ingramcontent.com/pod-product-compliance
Lightning Source LLC
Chambersburg PA
CBHW071554080326
40690CB00056B/2037